Independently published by *Driftwood Press*
in the United States of America.

Managing Poetry Editor:
Sara Moore Wagner
Cover Design: Sally Franckowiak
Covers & Interior Images: Leigh Viner
Innards Design: James McNulty
Copyeditor: Sara Moore Wagner
Fonts: Rift Soft, Maecenas, Garamond,
& Merriweather

Copyright © 2025 by Clayre Benzadón
All Rights Reserved.

No part of this publication
may be reproduced, stored in a retrieval
program, or transmitted, in any form or by
any means (electronic, mechanical,
photographic, recording, etc.), without
the publisher's written permission.

First published on September 30, 2025
ISBN-13: 978-1-949065-38-1
Please visit our website at www.driftwoodpress.com
or email us at editor@driftwoodpress.net

PRAISE FOR
MOON AS SALTED LEMON

"In these vulnerable, seeking poems, Clayre Benzadon queers and queries language, the body, desire, and identity to map and rewild the self and the selves Jewish, Spanish, Floridian, Queer, Daughter, Lover—that converge in this singular speaker. Here, intellect and wordplay are the tools that enable these poems to twine, slippery and playful, toward a more complex, embodied truth. For this reader, *Moon as Salted Lemon* is an opportunity to reconnect with language's subversive powers."

— Elizabeth Bradfield,
author of *SOFAR* and *Cascadia Field Guide: Art, Ecology, Poetry*

"What I love most is when a poet can show me the world I think I know in fresh, uncompromising ways: the 'asterisk body,' the 'bovine sky,' the 'heat' in 'heathen' and the 'moth' in 'month.' Clayre Benzadon's debut collection, *Moon as Salted Lemon*, brims with sharp analogies, 'valiant juices,' and 'poached vulnerability.' It's as visceral as a pucker, as nimble as a climbing vine."

— Julie Marie Wade,
author of *Just an Ordinary Woman Breathing*

"In her debut collection, *Moon as Salted Lemon*, Clayre Benzadon delights in breaking down binaries—gender, sexuality, pain/pleasure, dream/reality, and language itself (seamlessly braiding English and Spanish). Full of gorgeous wordplay, *Moon as Salted Lemon* explores Benzadon's Sephardic lineage, her feminist rage, recipes, word problems, and abracadabra... She offers us a book full of surprise and wonder."

— Denise Duhamel,
author of *Second Story*

"This stunning debut collection is a multilingual poetic manifesto that advocates for a fierce scrutiny of the institutions that raise us. These poems remind me that authentic belonging to family, faith, and self is difficult and vital work. Benzadón cracks open words to find new meanings with linguistic agility and a reserve of compassion that leaves me in awe. These poems answer poetry's highest call—to make and remake language—and as readers we are nourished and revitalized by her dedication."

— Mia Leonin,
author of *Unraveling the Bed*

"Clayre Benzadón's debut poetry collection delivers a time-warping, globetrotting, multilingual adventure in queer, Hispanic, and Jewish American experience. Fearless in its confessions, daring in its formal innovations, and true to its title, *Moon as Salted Lemon* contemplates both the tart and the luminous portions of the self. In this, Benzadón's poems are richly nostalgic, introspective, and sensual, but perhaps most impressive of all, they are as keenly relatable as they are original."

— Jaswinder Bolina,
author of *English as a Second Language and Other Poems*

For my family, friends, therapists, (treatment center) peers, advisors, mentors, Brandeis community, and the University of Miami MFA program. Thank you also to the Casa Ana Writing Residency and the Sundress Academy for the Arts for providing me the uninterrupted space and time to write, research, and more dauntingly, allowing me to reorganize (obsess) over other versions of my manuscript.

To Maureen Seaton, the kindest, funn(i)est, most positive queer spirit who changed my life, helped me find my (queer feminist) voice, and consoled me like a mother angel soul, loving me, pushing me, and challenging my mindset throughout many of life's discomforts.

CONTENTS

I.

MOON AS SALTED LEMON	3
WHEN THE ROOT OF APPLE (חופת) SWEETLY EXHALES	5
SER LA LECHE	6
LEMON AS ETROG / THE GROWTH AND SWALLOW OF A JEWISH MOM'S PHENOMENOLOGICAL BODY	8
PANIC ATTACK	9
HORNBONE SEASON	11
WHEN A DREAM SPEAKS TO ME	12
BIOLUMINESCENT INSOMNIA	15
QUÉ GUAY	17
NASOPHILIA	20
ORANGE SOMATICS	22

II.

THRUM	27
LA FÁBUL(OS)A	28
LEMON: A PRELUDE	30
HUNGERING OVER / SOLIDIFYING INTO SUCCADE	31
SURREAL ARCHITECTURES	35
NO ME IMPORTA UN PIMIENTO	36
7 INGREDIENT (WAY TO WISH FOR SOMEONE'S JUST DESSERT) LEMON BAR RECIPE	39
CATEGORY THEORY	41
NIMBLE / THIMBLE TOUCH	45
THE FUCKED UP PART ABOUT FUCKING YOU	46
SLEIGHT OF HAND	48

III.

THE OPPOSITE OF LIMELIGHT	53
BALANCEANDO	56
SEPHARDIC SHABBOS STARVED	59
WHY ARE THERE BOUNDARIES	67
I. EX NIHILO (EXILIO)	70

STATELESS	71
LADINO	73
KABBALISTIC HAUNTINGS	76
BLOOD LIBEL	79
II. DREAM PHANERON	82
FACETS OF CONTROL OF CONTROL / I'M STILL TRYING TO FIGURE OUT / MY EX'S PARTNER / HOW TO CHILL OUT	83
ARS POETICA #___	87
HOW TO COMPLETE A MEAL / HOW TO MAKE MYSELF FULL (WHOLE)	90
LINGUISTIC REWILDING / REBOBINAS LINGUÍSTICOS	95
INTERVIEW: BETWEEN SURVIVAL & ERASURE	101

MOON AS SALTED LEMON

tonight I wedge
the moon
into bottom
of glass

con cada luna llena

watch it erupt
leak teal

*cuando llega
el atardecer*

I can't squeeze
Julieta Venegas'
"Limon Y Sal" out

of my head
only Clase Azul
finger-

tip swirling
salt around
the rim

of a shotglass

Evening brings out
the bluest part

almost half
of this lemonmilk

body is salted
by silicon

dioxide glass
created by meteoroids

hitting it

WHEN THE ROOT OF APPLE (חופת) SWEETLY EXHALES

separate the skin / from the apple /
manzana / sounds like mechitza /
mitzvah / it is a good deed /
to separate / his meat / from her milk

SER LA LECHE

Gutpunch as soon as the soap-sour aroma touches the two front teeth, buoys creamy, full-bodied, at the roof of the mouth, gurgle-clogs the throat with foam.

O sea, *mala leche*. Si tomas leche así, del carton, y sabe podrida: mala suerte, sabes?

As in, I am the milk, like I am the shit, *sick*, in liquid form— take me as I am.

Cuando te doy una leche, it's a gesture towards sweetness, sis, I'm thinking of the juxtaposition of the phrase "don't cry over spilled milk", and how the tongue is naturally more sensitive to dulce (de leche) when things are hotter (like me, when I want to be).

I'm thinking more of the spilling as useful, a tactic, pouring a glass of it over your head: *here, have this milk, drink it, bit(ch)* of milk magic (like Milk Bar®, or the makeup company).

Sometimes, the sourness begins to froth when mom or dad tells me, "estás de mala leche hoy", or especially when remembering the taste of the off-white liquid protein substitute they used to make me gulp down—I'd hold my nose every time I had to ingest a tablespoon of artificial lemon, a toxic I'd almost puke back into the amber bottle—

For dad, the most important part of a child's growth involved strong bones: his reminder, *proteína*! sounded like the *got milk?* campaign, but to advertise Cola Cao Chocolate Drink Mix instead; worst would have been to have a son who ended up *enclenque*, weak, feeble, lanky...

I lap up what I can get, I guess; see, I am the milk because the body inhabits what it's most averse to. Milk is the food of the gods, the first human diet, yet galactosemia means something else: galactose + blood, or the accumulation of galactose in my blood, the inability to properly metabolize sugar into the galactic—in this way I unshapen, travel all the way down to the gut, then eventually collect in the liver.

Sí, soy la leche. Maybe I'm milking it, but my instincts tell me I've been that lost boy on the milk carton for so long, people finally know who I am: except I'm not the proud son, I don't have the muscle for it. Sometimes it meant I was the schoolkid without a proper birthday party (I couldn't have my cake, and I couldn't eat it either).

> *Women tend to have smaller, thinner bones than men.*

I'm trying to metabolize this fact. I'm churning it. No matter what form the milk surfaces as, maybe all I'm reaching for, wading towards, is to reach kin above the milk skin, to form into nata, a delicacy soft to taste, melt-in-the-mouth digestible.

What it really boils down to is this:

more than I try to skim
/ the girl out myself,

more than anything,

> I'm the (m)ilk
> / of my mother.

LEMON AS ETROG / THE GROWTH AND SWALLOW OF A JEWISH MOM'S PHENOMENOLOGICAL BODY

My mother stands in the kitchen while my father
hunches over the table, cuts an orange
swirls the skin with his control
of serration (silence of sawscrape)—

(dad's) offhand remark: "la religion judía solo sirve
a los hombres."

—

My mother mimics Martha Rosler's
rendition of "Semiotics of the Kitchen",
stabs the air with a fork / fork with grater,
slams the tenderizer onto the table.

—

Father moves to the couch, the siddur
hiding his face as he dozes off.

Mother is still
making noise, a mess,
studies for the LSAT

while she beats
a lemon
meringue paste.

PANIC ATTACK

after Joanna Newsom's "Only Skin"

Only skin it is only skin
but it feels like a sharp

string knotted around
    my wrists

  outside of myself
    is dissonance
      mute voice
      dissociation

        I lie down for
        sixteen minutes—

I have to close my body
but softly, because when I do
 it's constant clenching,

asterisk body latticed
through my bedroom
rug

a harmless shaggy
corpse a cover
for panic

At fourteen, enclosed
in a fur coat, I'm running off
with someone on a cruise

After my family
finds me
I guilt trip

gulping to the point
of panting for air

about to vomit
and my heart
        my heart blooms
        beneath
        vein of feather-
        weight
        frame—

Skin is
as malleable
as scraps
of sassafras

so easy to burrow
into like yarrow

and it is an addiction
to be a woman
who   strips off
        her body,
        peels it
  off in
an attempt   to detach from
  the past of
        skin.

HORNBONE SEASON

We grow   horns and bones

to/get/her   her and I

    sin   rest   tame

     in even order

 by   eve   ice

   erodes   dolorido

     en verano   summer is sore

de / sol / ate   sol   skin the sun thin

fino   si / no   rouse a sour rose

delay its flourish   lay above

it puzzle the swimming gar/den

a bovine sky   vying for luck

for her season   her heat/hen

      temporada de parpadeos

     huesos   I crave   you

give   me / meat /   meet   me at

el cuerno   / carnal / calor es su

vida (la subida) /   eres   corporal

WHEN A DREAM SPEAKS TO ME

I keep dreaming of you,
your almost numerical
face, the way it dots

with boldness, loose
vintage polka-dot blouse,
pulled into your jeans—

you're always tucking
a game of phrases
into your pocket,
bringing them with you:

that's the
the tea, the anti-
thesis

of subtle meanings
left behind, illusory.

Illustrated in ungrounded
territory: sky-tethered
elevator. Inside,

I wanted to distract myself
from the claustrophobia—

but by grabbing you
by the shirt-
pocket

against
metal

making out
with you as you
knot my tie up
at the throat—

once the doors
open, you retreat,
opposite direction,
before I even have

a chance
to wake up—

how am I supposed to read you
when the note you leave on my dash,
months after says, *you know who it is.*

You are a moth striped in ripples at
the intersection of myself. A mimicry,
geomagnetic. You don't eat.

> (In my dream
> I fast
> for you)

Months pass like moths. You re-speak
to me with swift touch—that's
when I would wish to wade into the rill

of you. But that night, in the dream,
you'd change the phrasing: *you know me,*

 don't know?

releasing your teeth (sarcastically
or sexily?)

        Well, do I?

Your face is a torn-up letter
I keep dreaming of,

a numerical atlas/
      moonmoth
I'll not ever be able to decipher.

BIOLUMINESCENT INSOMNIA

The next night
is a vacated

stain the tone
of coal

a print that lasts
flammable

earth-
worn

worm crawling
through its hydro-

skeleton

respiring through
its skin

naked as buck-
wheat sprouting

bioluminescent
nectar

outside dim is (h)eatless
ready to light-

starve evening
with luciferin

it resists the
click beetle

its snap of body halves
a cricket racketing

deep enough

to teem the ground
luminous

QUÉ GUAY

I.

In the backyard of Madrid summer,
unpatterned patchwork embeds turf.

My cousins and I are chasing bees
outside their house, whacking

the creatures with tennis rackets.
The fissured organs look sprightly to me.

I think that to gain dominion over
something that can sting me

is righteous. Fuzz and thorax
punctures from its abdomen.

White foam spurts out.
Froth from the pool laps at our feet.

We are above the tile, on top of
a boulder, about to cannonball in.

II.

Enanito! The older brother calls
to his younger one. I laugh. I like

him a little too much. The little one
starts to sing Selena's "Como la Flor"

in a pleasant pre-pubescent pitch.
Ma-ri-co-co-co, his brother serenades

III.

back to him. Nature feels nimble,
   como manos de madrugada,

organized fissures to suffice
the gore of matching machismo,

of the older one's word: *maricón*.
Como *maduro, o masticar*.

Faggot—It's a throttled swallow,
marcado adentro del órgano vital, corazón

como una maleta llena de masculinidad,
  una máscara sin sentimiento.

The forced pouring, the push into
the water. The boys play-tackle in the pool.

Se enfrentan mientras se bañan en la espuma.
It's the gayest thing I've ever seen.

NASOPHILIA

It's a good thing straws
are too wide to fit
inside a kid's nose

because at camp
all the kids wanted
to stick crayons

up their cavities
or super glue their
nostrils together,

like the 18-year-old
female presented
in a 2015 case study titled

"Deliberate Self-
Harming Application
of Superglue

in the Nose: Case Report
/ Literature Review,"

to avoid
having a nasogastric tube
up her septum,

and the sea turtle in Costa
Rica that had scientists
pulling a straw out of its nostril—

estoy hasta las narices
con todo esto, up to my noses,
up to *here* while reading
through damaging case
studies, the 150 million

tons of plastic
that currently flow
through the ocean,

the presentpresent-
ationperformance
as teacherjewoman

feminine (who even knew
the etymology of this word
comes from "to suckle?")

in the middle
of making a gay poem,
Freud barges in to interpret
the nose as a substitute
for penis

(does anxiety even breathe?)

well, thank the patience
of erek appayim,
my partner's kink
is *long [of] noses*

I hadn't ever focused
on the freckle
at the tip of my own

until she pokes it.

ORANGE SOMATICS

I was never instinctive enough;
took your blood
orange by the slice.

I had to use a knife
to skew its rind.

Peel through example.
Slit a nail through its navel,

    midsweet,

  sip the top,
then spit out the pips.

Now try it on me.

When you licked my stomach
button, I touched the blade
to your nose to test

its bluntness.
You didn't think
to withdraw.

I drew you with my tongue
enough times to forget food,

almost stabbed you
with my hunger,
which only exists since

I've learnt it
through my body.

Somatics are semantic:
you squeezed the color

orange, full of rage,
out of me so hard

I ignited, sensitive:

I (be)came pulp
and laved myself

near my navel

with valent
    juices.

THRUM

You are harmless without antlers,
rare amidst hard tusk-teeth, raiding
essence of alpine, lichen, a musk

fang puncturing
the small muscle

of a poached
vulnerability.

LA FÁBUL(OS)A

Xana does not think of holding her stomach before falling asleep every night, imagining the myth of a pulse, mariposa nadando in the liquid of herself. Her waist is a sacred hearth, hourglass-shaped, a form warmed and reserved only for her.

There is no friction in it, only the fiction of what she might conjure up: ranas (*xana, xana, culito de rana*, the giants of her town would tease her with, replacing the beginning letter "s" of "sana" with "x", her name only serving as placeholder), snake-dragons, ventolinas... she imagines the wind on her face recovering her past, her path of her body, which bends idle underneath the god, or goblin, or some other sort of creature, who wants to feel her.

Xana stays for him, in bed, restless, even after the paranoia— *please protect me*, she's telling him, but really praying as she watches the ceiling the whole time he continues to pound into her—myth is disposable, the body is disposable, the way she trembles—(she starts to see stars: xxx)—it's how her body responds when she is about to dissociate—

Myth is a way to avoid memory, a confiscation. The lords of storms, los nuberos, tell her trauma is a myth, repossess her reality of her long-lost mythological birthing, her imagination, her image, the gods cross out x's on her stomach, hex her with a shame that internally flurries a dragonfly soft enough to butter her stomach.

What ends up growing inside of her is botanical, blossom of frogs, births moonbeam and lovewater. This mystical force helps her fit through the keyhole of her house, enters with a stealth that helps her rewrite, recover that small x she'd been seeing everywhere, through gaps of architecture, in the apertures of her ribs, in the crossing "y" of "myth"—the fábula turns fabulosa once she uncovers the myth of language— "x" is versatile, a phonetic chameleon, mysterious precision, it's life and death. The gods end up crucifying her, burning her at the stake of exaltation—the rest of town crowns her in death with a wreath of angel's trumpet and dandelion seeds, then she is designated in the sky as the most eternal and experimental of stars.

LEMON: A PRELUDE

A lemon listens for when it's listless,
a taste like a worthless hand-me-down,

a suck-the-syrup out of pulp
fiction, or a lemon-zappy type

fanzine, where I sip
and imbibe and draw

and still wait for the sex
to come seeping, like

a Sussex pond pudding
oozing with sweat, suet,

a whole sun
in its middle.

HUNGERING OVER / SOLIDIFYING INTO SUCCADE

Back in Florida,
no room for fall.

I've learnt to neglect
all indications
of changing

seasons since
college.

The colors
of my mother's cayenne
sprinkles, dashes

of turmeric powdering
branches of cauliflower

wouldn't, at any time, be as vivid
as Massachusetts foliage

and I was thankless
enough to look out the window

rather than at my mom
when she served me a plate,

and to mash the florets
until they melted a burnt

rust—Miami felt
like it had decayed,

and so had I,
inside the city—

tiny sizzles
grew louder

from outdoor heat,
from our kitchen—

how I hungered
for autumn, clean
pulps of snow.

Sometimes boundaries
are set to mark seasons.

I was looking for that,
for another space. I hid

my simmer while my mother
heightened stove heat,

pot boiling quicker each
dinner, when she'd dish

me up and I'd twirl the food
on my plate, still gazing

off in starvation, in far-
sickness.

My mom eventually stops
cooking. We both cease
eating. I remain

in my room. She stays
hunched

over her desk.
We thin in distance.

The periphery between
us divides the tiled

hallway from my parent's
bedroom carpet.

While my mom sleeps,
I slip a letter to her
under her door.

In the lined margin
I scribble: *I'm sorry,
mom. I did not mean
to confine us.*

*I only wanted to
confide in you;
I miss
you.*

I've already left the house
by the time she wakes.

She sits out on
the lawn bench,

flushed with saffron,
peach, imperceptible threshold—

in the canal underneath
her, the one she studies,
my face appears.

We meet. When I dimple,
it is hers. There's a silent
simplicity that mirrors.

I tread closer, then settle
down next to her with
a secret clasp of lemon peels.

Even the shell of this fruit
can't tolerate low
temperatures, but here

they bud,
continuously.

I wrap one around
her hair like a scrunchie,

then scrutinize it
candying in the sun.

SURREAL ARCHITECTURES

I'm grateful for the room
with pines and their spines
that brush my face like a coyote

lapping at transient berries,
their lupine shadings
in the holographic.

The modern is normal.
Sometimes this means igloos
seep through the bricks

of this eonic pen
conking out nocturnality.

Sometimes it means to serve
little owls and lizard fish their
benthic freeswims, scaleless
woodland fringes.

When I think of the precision
of coo, I think of a pigeon
wearing a lollipop choker,

its synecology,
a soft sucking.

NO ME IMPORTA UN PIMIENTO

When my aunt and uncle
come to visit, my Tío goes,
"Esperamos fiesta,"

"we're waiting for you to get
married"— I play with my necklace
pendant with an engraving

of "The Lovers" tarot card,
(the one you gave me, babe,
with two women on it)

and stare at the EXIT sign—

I want to be as bold
as you, to stand up

   and command
I don't care one pepper

in front of family, or every-
one else,

  I'd love to believe it,

to openly hold the weight
your spice carries, pop you

in my mouth like dragon's
breath, scald myself while

devouring you,
a devil's tongue,

in public, and not
give a fuck

about the furrowed-
brow, squinty-eyed,
spiced reaction.

So what if
back at the restaurant

I look too american,
off-the-derech—

babe, miénteme,
invert me like a pimenta
obscura (threatened
species),

teach me how to bite
a habanero
whole, by the stem,

enough to heat and mute
my ears to the rest of
the conversation

(I'd love to add
some zest
to my life any-
way),

then show me

como ser
fresca, seasoned,
fearless.

Right now, I wish
I could rage
right through the exit,

but the only
way I know how

to display sauciness
is by drenching
    myself in it.

7 INGREDIENT (WAYS TO WISH FOR SOMEONE'S JUST DESSERTS) LEMON BAR RECIPE

*What you will need: Butter, sugar, vanilla extract, salt, eggs, lemon juice

1. **Immerse** (yourself in the idea that) hand in sugar and salt (sweet means leave) melted butter (flatter me lavishly) and vanilla (with husks of plainness) concoction.

2. **Feed** flour to the mix. (Feed it, the leftovers). Let sticky harden onto hand. **Note:** The dough will be thick. (Heavy is the hand that kneads [needs] it).

3. **Firmly press** the crust into pan (I don't allow room for a creamy massaging, or air bubbles). After it bakes, **poke** holes over top of crust.

4. **Sift** sugar (grit) and flour (finest part of) together to make the base of filling. Whisk eggs (foolish pies, thrown in your face [imaginatively speaking]), then the lemon juice (I'll hand it to you), until fully combined (you look good yo[l]ked together with that other warm structure you crunch, gnash in your jaws, that hot hot crust, you smirk at me while you eat it).

5. **Pour** filling over crust. **Bake** the bars for 25 minutes, or until the center no longer jiggles. (**stop** wiggling around—don't worry, I'll admit, the half-baked pastry tastes even better).

6. **Remove** the bars from the oven and let them completely cool (give them some time to stop being so angry). Once cool, **lift** the parchment paper out of the pan (you never did know the meaning of gentle). **Dust** with confectioners'

sugar and cut into squares (**rub** the lemon square's face off, cause an uproar). **Wipe** the knife clean between each cut (you never did know the meaning of clean-cut)...

7. **Identify** me (thawed). **Serve** me this way.

CATEGORY THEORY

Identity is defined
with the purpose of serving
an object.

For every object X,
there exists
a morph-

ism id$_x$ (now trans-
form it psychologically,

satisfy my id understated,
my unconscious purpose
to understand ideas).

An object is an idea.

I am the object.

*

Word Problem*: you're sitting outside the Starbucks on campus, by yourself, minding your own business, when a random dude (x) comes up to you and tells you you look like someone whose got the Vans and look of someone who works at Hot Topic.

1. After this encounter, what would you **categorize** yourself as?

2. What was the **function** of this confrontation?

    * (why "word" and not "math"?)

What does it mean to function? to purpose, propose, prevail intending towards a person,

thing, or relationship involving one or more variables?

How to function as object: transfigure into shape (determined as external form or appearance characteristic of someone or something: the outline of an area or figure.)

*

1. I'd categorize myself
as the carcass
of a concave triangle,
abject, an object of trauma.

2. There is no way
to function
in this state.

*

Let me go back
to origin-
ality:

the etymology of "define"
comes from "to specify; to fix
 or establish authoritatively".

The mapping of patterns,
categories, attempts to
determine figures,

symmetry,
is natural.

   *

So is correlating
disorder in psychological
terms. For instance,

triangulation can be mathematical
but can also occur when
an outside person intervenes

to manipulate
the shape
of an interaction.

   *

Or, let's refer back to the object
of x, but this time,
a different man—

at work, I have the responsibility
of teaching x how to operate
language. He asks me:

"why do you have such short hair?
I mean, you're pretty,
but you'd be even more beautiful

if it was longer;
thought you'd cut it

because you got
gum in it or somethin' "—

*

(questioning < intrusiveness
half angle identity ≠ bi [imagine number bi
   is $-b^2$; assume hetero-
       normativity])

*

To what extent has the supernatural
quality of this X-man savior complex
rescued me from myself?

He existed in a bounded function
of authority, delineates pure imaginary
numbers (i)

to assume the value 0
   (i [me] =0; [zero is considered to be
       both real and imaginary])

until I proof the equation
wrong; rewrite the root of

of identity from "sameness"
to "entity":
   i= radical
multiplicity
   surface of a revolution

NIMBLE / THIMBLE TOUCH

In full sun, or cold
tolerance, asters grown in, all

charmed and untoothed, wild—
their star-slit petals cross

each other, aster-

isks, ticks, tisks
of remembrance.

There is a game
blossoms play

with each other:

besides the speckled
throats, plants choose

to dress, protect them-
selves in fox-

glove sleeves, thimbles,
during a game of tag, or touch

-me-not—
a half-life lasts a day.

I stare at the aster,
at its last finger of

pulverized breath.
It sheathes, sneezes

like a collapsed core
of a black hole.

THE FUCKED UP PART ABOUT FUCKING YOU

It's only when
I'm on top

that I get to control
my view,
motion: there

is an uncanny
tidiness about you:

glossed back
forehead, raven
-deep eyes, spiked

grizzle hair that pulls
in one direction.

I want to pull it,
but you grab my hands
down before

I can get to
whining, you put

my mouth
over my hand.

Don't
cry

but now
that's all
I want to do—

like a girl again—
begging.

You hold my head down,
a doctor sticking a tongue
compressor down the throat.

You slap my face
with the ruler:

Good
girl,

demand I make myself bare
for you, without hair,
without protection.

The creased smile
that always touches
your lip is formidable.

I linger too long
on your musculature,
of all the ways you could
crush me.

I love it
when you
hurt me.

SLEIGHT OF HAND

my nails are a rasp
that fractures the thicket

of impulse makes
my knuckles
bleed

resistance
is so limp
how do I stop

myself from hurting
myself with my hands

the act of digging
myself out feels
 mythical jolted

this is a test
of self-control

precision of hand
means something different
when my fingers want to

curl up like a raven's
claw ravenous
scarring uninhibited

have you
ever watched
a berry bleed
 so feebly

it looks so vivid
    free   raw

to dissociate
     i etch
her out so she
can reach
out for her
  missing physical-
                        ities

THE OPPOSITE OF LIMELIGHT

Who cares about that lime-
glimmer, all ragged and exclamatory?

Its spark can turn slanted,
invert as lemonlucent lantern instead.

Theme song: Led Zeppelin's "The Lemon
Song". I take them out from the box,

those little rolled-up Meyer matches,
turn the lemonheads upside-down,

like my own metal head
heavy to the drum-bass thrash—

till the juice runs down

and my hands run lighter
now, consist of match(ing)
fingers.

Limes of light
line my tip,

not burnt out, but

stale flames which combust
after I pick a guitar

numb to the neck-fret,
"Fingers On Fire"

(Arthur ["Guitar Boogie"] Smith)
next, dimmed in the background,

not loud or as literal as musician
Davidlap's lapdance with his

lapping fireshow, twirling
incandescence, but more

of a carburizing wring)\)\)
now take it down a little bit)\)\)

With my pinky, I skim
my lemon sheet (cake),

char the sown outwear
of the electrochemical

neon sponge-candy
furniture (then twist

my lips in amusement,
to discover that my hands

have turned into Lemonheads™!)

The limelight
 attempts to exhume free

radicals,

those molecular fragments
with a short lifetime.

Now I backmask the song
(reversal play):

a lime can turn
yellow when over–

ripe, and lemons
greens when underripe.

The key lime
ingredient is this (sublime):

(*I should have quit you, baby*)

My lemon self doesn't want
the limelight; instead my tangy

batteries turn inward, save
the saturated tea for other hot attention.

BALANCEANDO

Pointillist rain scatters, drenches
me in rain mid-
flight. I'm five years old

as my father lullabies to me
in the backyard playground:

un elefante balanceando
sobre la tela—

I'm swinging on a young net,
learning to balance, my father

next to me, como primeros pasos,
como si estuviera andando—

already I was
    risky
with wanting—

I imagined striding
atop the swing set

as seamlessly as a tight-
rope walker, or like *Babar*

and the Adventures
my dad would read to me,

when the elephant floated
on air balloon.

At six, I trusted my father
to let go of me
without training

wheels.
I slipped off of
my bike,

kept falling every
time after.
The scars on my
knees stung,

but I determined
to hurt myself

until I could ride
without handle
bars—

como veía que resistía—

I have a recurring vision
that my father runs towards
me

as I arrive at the top
of a skate ramp.

I look down
beyond my board,

quivering, practically
backwards.

He's far ahead of me,
waving his hands
towards me.

I land, catch speed,
catch up to him—
when we intersect—

hay deslizamiento; I slip—
footpace inch of distance—

lapse inside realm of home.
My father and I are standing
right near the living

room door. When we
say goodbye—

dame un beso,
he motions—

I barely get
enough air to
reach his cheek.

SEPHARDIC SHABBOS STARVED

Anchovies and sardines
all folded and oiled inside,
tin-can-cramped,

sopa de lentejas, ajo,
bone marrow sucked
dry, chewy salt-luscious

core, best part of adafina stew
every Shabbat lunch:
(beans, browned translucent

potatoes, onions, speckled
hard-boiled egg),
an artichoke prickling

impregnable thumbprint,
pickled lemons, aceitunas,
roscones (the ones

my brother could
never shape,
my aunt empathically

laughing at his flailing
determination)—

*

After my parents found
out I had Galactosemia,
they fed me on a strict

mango-only
diet (*strict* is meant
to protect

when it's
the only thing
you know).

*

When it's the only
thing you know:

10 years old.

Saturday synagogue
youth group.

I play basketball
with the twins

I've been crushing
on for too long.

There's a new couple
who runs the program.

The woman sits outside
the swing outside

her home. I stand
watching her, amused

by what looks to be
a mouth(ful) / guard,

an elongated, sunburst-
parrot sticky-luscious

treat.

she hands
me a slice,

asks me
about want.

*

The tang's dangerous;
I keep drawing it in
with nips of my teeth.

Amba, melon, it could
have even been star-
fruit, or leems,

leaning onto
preserved
pulp.

A rind-reigned smile
is directed toward me.
(Sorry for the overdone

duplication. Sorry
for *sorry*. I hate
to generalize, but Jews

tend to go through
apologies as repetitive
as prayer).

*

Kiddush prayer:
Dad holds a gold
chalice of wine,

or grape juice while singing
the rendition reminiscent
of the lingering

chord progression in Stone
Temple Pilot's "Interstate
Love Song" ("only yesterday

you l-I-I-I-ED").

*Promises of what
I seemed to be.*

What did I seem
to be?

A little girl
ambitious to try
all that I could:

when my tío
came over for Saturday
Sabbaths, he'd open a can

of anchoas, the surprise
a noise that popped open,
he'd cut a slice of mojama,

give me that knowing eye-
brow raise, *te gusta comer
todo, no?* and I'd nod my

head fervently, I needed it
to be made known that
I could practically consume

the whole world, if given
the chance (dairy excluded)—

sometimes, I pretended that
slices of tortilla de patata

were pizza, and I kept
claiming it, *I'm eating pizza,*
so happy with the fantasy,

the freedom, and my dad
kept correcting me. I became
consumed, I couldn't

stop eating it, it was
delectable; I got so sick.
Just like when I vomited red

and wasn't sure if it
was from watermelon
(like the one my young brother

dropped in the middle
of the Spanish grocery store,
the splatter another

cackle my aunt let out)
or the hot dog I ate,
(I'd just seen a movie

where a character named
Frankie gets sick from a frank-
furter and I couldn't

get the image out
of my mind).
As ill as when I cried

hard enough to hurt
my stomach whenever
my parents left me

with the babysitter
to go on dates,
and the song my mom

would sing me to sleep
when she came back was
The Sound of Music's

"My Favorite Things":

Cream-colored ponies
and crisp apple strudels
Doorbells and sleigh bells
and schnitzel with noodles.

*

Noodles as warmth.
As (family) business.
Taken from another
culture.

Cuisine as control.
Diet as restraint,
Galactosemic

Kosher cost of it
all. The luxury
of nightly

home-cooked
dinners.

In the end,
my brother became
the most successful

and dedicated to food.
A sourdough connoisseur,
committed to koji pedagogy.

In his adolescent, he
was a picky eater. As
soon as his teens, as soon

as he stopped adhering
    to the hard-
boiled, rigid-set meal

rules (*strict* is meant
to protect),

he became
free to ingest
adventure,

and I, I'm
still fastened
and folded and

oiled inside a tin-
can-cramped casket,
like The Hungry Cater-

pillar, I'm perpetually
attempting to eat
the entire earth.

WHY ARE THERE BOUNDARIES

dividing line   _____   limit

furthest   point

with / in   degree   thresh /
                                                          hold

           decree   *you can*

                                  have it

bound by the wrists

                          how sexy

                                                 to be cornered

               of course

to be held   *gripped*

               you said   *be straight*

                                    with me

you were always   *in my corner* |

                              cracked

protective | you meant | *possessive*

            occupy
                                          inhabit

                        space
                                                my mind

            hold in | control |
                                              master of my
                        own
    head   *yes*

                    yes
                                            I don't

                              speak

| *please* |

no | no |

no no so

two letters

are harsher

than (>) |3|

thank you

for bleeding
---------------- ~~the lines~~ ----------------

between you

and | I |

between

myself

and I

I. EX NIHILO (EXILIO)

"Intrigue taunts my
heart like a pennant

on a ships' mast, in a storm;

and exile is ink
in God's book
across my soul and every shore;"

[...]

"So I said: This is me—
for I, too, am in exile,
far from my family and friends.
In exile, you have grown tall,
and alike we're far from home"

— Schmuel HaNagid (lines taken from "A Curse" and from *Selected Poems of Shmuel HaNagid*)

STATELESS

Of course, Spain
was not a country
for immigrants.

We Jews, we didn't
get to choose, we just
ended up stateless.

It makes sense
that we're so good
at hiding

god behind us.

Ladino
is our crypto-
gram, our first

romance,
our old Spanish.

We were never meant
to speak. To admit

Jews was to attack
the very essence
of Span / ish / ness.

All these qualifiers:
ish. Span-ish. Jew-

ish. Ness: נס.
Meaning miracle.

Where was the clear
marvel embedded

in the span
of a pain-

slurred country.

Expulsion is an old
pulse that always slips
and its ghosts are still

living.

In the late nineteenth century
[...] knowledge of Jews
among the majority

of Spaniards was non-
existent—

the Sephardic
tradition is to name
one's children after
living relatives.

I'd like to believe
it's the wind that asks,

is it time for the Jews
to leave
~~Europe~~?

It whispers
Clara, Clara, Clara,
Cl-aire. Until

it anglicizes
into air.

LADINO

Vivíamos doble vida:

//

double life

//

Nosotros judíos estabamos expuestos al fenómeno políglota

//

lengua-

je   ab(sence)

suelta   sal-

vada

//

especialmente los que hemos tenido que emigrar más de una vez

//

ja-que-tía (ja, que tia, para dar me esta forma

dialectal)   *jaquetía*

(*ponga*

chaqueta is   a common

father saying [in Miami // el norte de Marreucos

(huecos)

a dónde   emigr-

amos?])

//

Esto nos genera algunas ansiedades sobra el idioma, o idiomas, particularmente cuando pensamos cuál deberíamos considerar nuestra lengua maternal [...]

//

judeo-

español lad i no / no pueden

ser judeo

si hablen   español

maiden language   laden in   la-di-no

canción

lenguaje bastarda   arcaico

hebreo   árabe

des a pari ción   ir rever sible

ex tin ción   scion   off

shoot

lag unas léxicas

//

la di   da   la di   día

las canciones que trajeron los sefardíes expulsados:

    víncula lingüístico   trans misión

        entre las generaciones

un imaginario sobre aquel país idealizado:

    ///////////////////////////////////////

        kaminos de leche i miel

KABBALISTIC HAUNTINGS

The word *abracadabra*
may have derived from

the Aramaic phrase:
"I will create as I speak",

or perhaps it's just
an abcedarian
for the destruction

of the future:
"perish like the word".

During World War II,
Late King Mohammed V
disintegrated the possibility
of defending

our humility: "we have no Jews
in Morocco, only
Moroccans",

and etymologically, the term "Jew"
inherently implies "person who
seeks gain by sordid means".

—

We magic the kabbalah,
jew-
el dream divination,

our collective
described as adjective:

*There is, in fact, a widespread
hesitation to describe Jews
as Jews.*

—

In 1950, there were more than
a quarter of a million Jews

In Morocco, but today
there are maybe 2,000,
in the big urban areas

of Casablanca and Marrakech,
land of god, land of journey,

The old country
remembers us.

Maybe once in a while
we transition to super-
stition, stitch

our pockets with
salt, but not while
wearing the coat,

open our umbrellas
in the house to invite

angelic essence
after pass-

over
mimouna festival

visit orchards
at nightfall

let us enchant
  ner tamid,
eternal flame

BLOOD LIBEL

Convert, depart, or die—

I would have
died for
a powerful gesture

of atonement—
it's what Jews
have been trained for,
attuned to—

Spain today has
one of the smallest
Jewish populations
in Europe:

*about 45,000
in a country
of more than*

*46 million
people.*

*Spain's centuries
of "silence
and oblivion" [...]*

*still haunt
the present:*

Franco names
the race

a disturbance
danger

—

Today a report
produced by Spain's
Observatory of Anti
Semitism found

that 58 percent
of the Spanish public
believes that "the Jewish
people are powerful

because they control
the economy
and the mass media."

To gain Sephardic
citizenship:

proof of Sephardic lineage,
rigorous, four-hour Spanish

language test
citizenship test

grave
deficiencies

Leave Salvador Espriu's
spirit, poem, on top
of my grave:

> [...]
> in the long
>   trail
> of your Exile—

(The Greek root of nostalgia,
nostos—means "return home."

More than an exercise
in nostalgia,
the longing for Sepharad

is a journey entangled
in violence [...]

forced conversion
trauma

sacrifice matar
judíos, that lemonade

and red wine
mix, spill it on me,
my memory,

call me dirty,
perra judía,
judiada

trick the juice
to become

the blood
of my own
soil.

II. DREAM PHANERON

*"Before my face, flowers, color which is form.
Cries plow the sea and air and turn to birth
Upon the people-sown, people-flowering earth.
A year turns in its crisis. In its sleep.
Whatever plows our dream is ours to keep."*

— Phaneron, Muriel Rukeyser

*"He'll bring you trouble with talk like dream,
invoking verse and song to cheat you;
but dreams, my son, aren't what they seem:
not all the poet says is true."*

— "He'll Bring You Trouble", Shmuel HaNagid

FACETS OF CONTROL / I'M STILL TRYING TO FIGURE OUT / MY EX'S PARTNER / HOW TO CHILL OUT

and as they'd walk out with him,
I'd still linger, waiting to know
if it'd be ok to kiss them last

because I'd been wanting to gnaw
on the semi-circle arrangement
of inked jasmine on their wrist,
the cat-lines of their eyes, a lash—

for so long.

Wednesday nights (liminal
existence), their husband
would come to pick them up
from my apartment and as

much as I'd appreciated the
you're so chill comments,
I would barely be able to keep

myself together— I'd be
wiggling my own knee,

which tingled
next to my ex's whenever
we sat on the couch—

later, we challenged
each other to see who could
hold a handful
of ice cubes longest.

My hand numbed
as I'd simultaneously
tried to tamp down

my electric
wetness

from a different
place.

I'd lost. "Stop
trying so hard",

they'd laugh
it off, then their partner

would arrive and
laugh at my red hand.

Then I'd turn red.

The first time he and I met
I extended my arms out

for a hug, but he fronted his
own up to shield himself.

"Stop trying so hard."
My ex had told me,

(I can't seem to stick
to any sort of form—

I wind up whining
about my own

passivity: "I'm sorry
for being over-
cautious; for thinking

the world will end
if I'm not constantly
moving"—)

so the next time I'd stick around
at the door, I'd stay cool, attempt

to copy a "Draw the Squad"
meme character configuration
they'd once shown me on their phone,

(*commit to your present
self*, we mottoed, even
laughed about it
in my car—

here I am,
in front of them again
from the perspective

of my car visor mirror,
where we both construct
ourselves, them watching

themselves reapply bruised
rouge while I self-

destruct, internally
chaoticize per-
form / (rom)ance,

attempt to stop
myself from charging

my fingers towards
them and wiping off
that microscopic

smudge of pink
from the corner of their lip)

while giving them a kiss
and their partner

    a backhand-
    ed high five.

ARS POETICA #_____

I was already thinking
about the future

of holding
the damn parts in place

(my arm, my breath,
your face):

the arm as practice
for blood drawn

because hospitals
scare me,

and I'm still clutching
my stomach,

breathe, you tell me
so I kiss you instead

(that's a practice
in halation of sorts)

before I catch
my throat thumping

as I merge
on the freeway

I've almost
fallen off

of you inches
away from bed

or your arm
has fallen asleep

from my back's

pressure on it

before it happens
it had already occurred

in my imagination
aren't I always

anticipating

"earnestly
desirous"

and isn't that
what I've been

trying to do this
whole time

through the full
unfolding

of this poem

persuading you

to lean

into the ladder
of me

escalate
scale

the most
heightened

catastrophes

and get you so
worked up

you'll end up
_____

HOW TO COMPLETE A MEAL / HOW TO MAKE MYSELF FULL (WHOLE)

Home-
made dinners every
night. The china

plates have been scraped
from so much use.
The dishwasher handle:

broken. My flank-rib-strip-
tease heart. The left-
overs, over-

flowing in the fridge,
I stuff myself (*make
myself whole*).

It's the way I complete
myself with lies. I'm full
of shit. Recovery:

a fabrication (I swear, I would
have preferred drugs to food).

Every day elapses,
the facility's window
a hidden sun visiting

my (vegetative) vegetable
body, a world-class
retreat.

*

*Morning munch.
Lunch. After-
noon snack.*

*Dinner.
Timed.
Hunger*

*cues, judge-
ment, I meant
binge,*

*restrict,
it's not to my
taste preference(s),*

*(I loved getting
to suck the flavor
out of my partner,*

*even if it drained
me to my ribbed-
hollow core:*

*please, people, I love people /
please! at least now I have
material for a hell-*

healthful poem).

*

Fuck cyan-eggshell
Miami balconies. I'm as
livid as swaying palm trees

that end up staying
in one place for rest

of their survival.

Complete / (meals) /
failure to launch;
gourmet plated,

*made whole, with
love*: I'm sorry
for spilling

mess.

*

The chaos
was my own
making:

haphazardly throwing
food, rushing to sprinkle
refrigerated shreds

of chicken onto plate,
leaving the counter sloppy
with poultry-putrid confetti,

every day a celebration
at the dinner table
while I hopelessly

eye my parents,
then direct gaze
towards my plate:

(DAD: *That's all
you're going to
eat? Gobble it up,*

*you're skeletal, as thin
as a Holocaust survivor*).
I was made

to believe
I'd been formed whole
and full and raven-

ous from food.
That was before.
I kept convincing myself

of a (false) narrative
of who I was, much
better version of a whole

rabbit, raw and boney,
displayed shamelessly,
without any more

dignity, or life left,
pink blob of creature
curled up on a tray.

*

The only *after* I could see
for miles was stained and
tainted flamingo pink, I was

lower on the food chain
than shrimp, filthy and

bottom-feeder-dependent
in behavior, sucking
up all selfless, sacred,

and satisfying spirits,
taking advantage
of my family's repetitive

dedication to cooking,
cleaning, feeding
(after) me, only for me

to throw away / clear
the sustenance off
of my path. This path

is a past, my last meal
(the Last Supper) will
only exist,

only emerge
when it ends

up leaving
me (whole).

LINGUISTIC REWILDING / REBOBINAS LINGUÍSTICOS

A dream as loose
as incomprehensible

wobbles like teeth
falling out depleted
like power outage

language cut
from gum   bomb/
   illa

trozos de carne asada
con sabor carnal   ass-
heavy

strong as la menta /
              la mente

encendida inside the mouth
like lengua   as automatic—

          *

Perra sucia.

With the replacement
of just a few letters

it's easy to convert
the vowel from "o"

to "a", to swap the sound
when it's convenient.

How can la libertad
be a woman when she is
      basura

      cocina
    doméstica
with the replacement
of just a few letters
letra / let her/
      roar

como una mujer man-
íaca, trapped, man-

tenida como un
trapo sucio,

manchada,
hasta que se convierte
en mugre.

      *

To preserve something
means to serve before
anything else,

to persevere with
the masculine standard
form. The language

regulator is Él, como
un padre quien me prescribe
mi rol de género:

eso no es como se sienta
una señorita,

    as if there
    were no room
    for women

    to feel. The "ita"
    is only added
    as a kindness

        *

I sit pretty, even when
"los hombres", used to
 mean "people",
  does not include me,

and "hembra" merely
refers to female animals,
stands in as slang for chick.

        *

When I'm a girl, I take the Spanish
into my mouth; it sparkles.
I leave my door open

when I change and my
father walks past me
as I strip into

a nude sparkler,
just like the words

I play with are,

bare in mi mano,
desnudos.

He barely sees me
but still flinches.

*

before he can say any-
thing,

 I yank my mouth
open with my tongue:

*voy hacer lo que
quiera como mujer,*

*y ella puede hacer
lo que le da*

*la gana con su
propio cuerpo,
lengua.*

*

I restore a remnant of
my tongue, my self—

the salvaje refuses
to leave me.

BETWEEN SURVIVAL & ERASURE
A CONVERSATION WITH CLAYRE BENZADÓN & SARA MOORE WAGNER

First, I want to shout an enthusiastic congratulations to you for winning our Editor's Prize. Your book stood out for its fire, sound, and meticulous research. We were all moved by the subject and originality of *Moon as Salted Lemon*. Let's start with the title. The image of the lemon runs through this collection, and you connect the image so well in your notes section. There's a focus on souring, especially in poems like "Ser La Leche," which juxtaposes the lemon with milk, which sours and curdles when lemon is introduced. What made the lemon such a central symbol, for you? It feels as complex and multifaceted as this collection!

Thank you so much! The title poem, "Moon as Salted Lemon" and Natalie Scenters-Zapico's collection *Lima::Limón* were the two pivotal works that really got me going in the direction of my obsession towards lemons. The focus of lemons is not only on the object itself but acts as a metaphor that serves as both a sweet and sour palate cleanser. The lemon is a symbolic representation that I choose to closely connect to religion, but which also serves as an imagistic mark that sets the stage for a budding feminist anthology. A lemon can be bright, tart, and acidic. Lemons are the basis for so many recipes; in that sense, lemons are crucial in our lives but seem to be placed in the background—that's another reason I choose to highlight them, to bring them to the foreground instead.

This book is a blending, a "queering," of so many things, culture, language, and the body. Before any of the poems, you call Maureen Seaton "the kindest, funn(i)est, most positive queer spirit," your "mother angel." How does her work inform this collection?

That's exactly right; Maureen Seaton encouraged the queering of forms in all definitions of the term "form" (she broke that idea apart in her workshop titled "Queering Forms"). When I think of Maureen's work, I think of play, of experimentation, of talking about sex and the body and the nature of the world, pop cultural references, and love, especially love. Maureen taught me the idea of risk: I hate math but she pushed me, in her gentle way, to go beyond the page. I did some learning on YouTube for how to solve a function, and that's where the poem "Category Theory" came about, thanks to Maureen. The lines I always come back to from her poem, "Sweet World" is this one: "[…] I never thought to call the world sweet before. / Surviving something can do that, make things taste different."

I love that idea of going to the places that are hardest, even if that's math. Could you tell us a little more about her definition of "Queering Form"? For instance, many of the poems in this book are exploring the body and gender identity in ways that are experimental and difficult to pin down, reflecting nonbinary identity in form and subject. I am so interested in the way you talk about the "Phenomenological Body" and gender performance and identity, both in your poems and in your notes section. Who are we beyond our bodies and beyond language? You say in "Orange Somatics," "Somatics are semantic." Could you explain your thoughts on this, and how the ideas of the phenomenological body and somatics inform your poetics, overall? Is this connected to that idea of queering form?

I believe beyond our bodies and beyond language, we are free, just as the idea of nonbinary identity is liberating. To me, the concept "somatics are semantic" refers to the idea that the way in which we inhabit a body is prescribed by the language that is used by society's (limited) perspective, usually one that is very black or white. If someone walks a certain way, dresses a certain way, they are automatically viewed as "feminine", "masculine", or if they don't fit the traditional roles assigned to them, they are considered "strange". I call the body "phenomenological" because one is constantly living in the body, experiencing the body, whether we want to or not, whether it's conscious or not. CA Conrad is one I turn to for thinking about the somatic practices of poetry (Maureen introduced us to them). One of CA Conrad's physical methods is using the body to act out or perform a ritual. My poem, "Panic Attack" is partly inspired by this prompt. Overall, I believe the written words, the material we have to release, are stored in the body, and are only partly let go once they're written on or beyond the page.

You use punctuation, slashes, and spacing in such interesting and experimental ways throughout this collection. How do you make those choices in your work? Does it come organically for you, or is it something that comes into focus in the later stages of revision? Does this connect, in any way, to your larger themes?

The use of unusual punctuation, slashes, and spacing does comes naturally for me. I think in this way, in such a messy, all-over-the-place sort of manner. In that way, the more experimental pieces kind of just come to me, especially for poems that hold a more complicated or big topic that I feel doesn't "fit" onto the page in the more traditional way that a poem might. In the later revision stages, I have to reign myself in, to create more consistency / make more sense of the spacing, for instance, as sometimes my choices are seen as arbitrary (and maybe they are, but again, these experimental voices are based mostly on impulse and intuition more than anything else). I believe the slashes and spacing does connect to my larger themes, which is mainly that of the queer, leaning into the "f*cking form" instincts that Maureen encouraged us to delve into.

Our current American administration is actively erasing nonbinary and trans identities. What do you wish people (people who are seeing their rights being stripped away, allies, and those who are working directly and indirectly to silence voices like yours) would take away from your book? Is the current political environment changing the way you write about this at all?

It's undeniable that our current American administration is actively erasing nonbinary and trans identities, and it's scary to be living in Florida these days because of it. I wish people (those who are seeing their rights being stripped away, allies, and those who are working directly and indirectly to silence voices like mine) would take away the fact that most importantly, my voice is not going away. I identify as both womxn and nonbinary, and my poetry is meant to disrupt / make the public feel uncomfortable, because I bring the "ugly", the truth, the reality of certain situations to the limelight. I also hope that queer folks can feel a sense of comfort while reading my book, and I hope that my experimental / multilingual style speaks to folks who have a difficult time expressing language in any other way.

The current political environment is absolutely changing the way I write about living and existence; my mentor and I are currently writing political poems both individually and in collaboration, and I've noticed a sort of shift in the way I write: more rhythmic, immediate, and even more dangerous.

I'd love to hear more about your process with mentors and collaboration, and your journey as a writer in general. How did you connect with your mentor? How important is it for the lit-

erary community that both new and established writers engage in mentor/mentee relationships? Do you have any advice for a writer who might want to seek out this kind of connection?

I'd say that my mentors have been pivotal in paving the way for my writing journey to go where it needed to lead me. My mentors have served as mirrors reflecting the truths that I needed to carve out for myself; they led me towards queerness, for example, or running towards the difficult topics that needed to be written about. I've been lucky enough to have connected with my mentor(s) first through college, at Brandeis, then later through my MFA program at the University of Miami. I think it's instrumental to the literary community that both new and established writers engage in mentor / mentee relationships, as the main lifeblood of poetry is community, and the love that comes about as a result of collaboration and shared vulnerable, raw, and creative energies that come about after writing and reading poems together.

When collaborating with my mentor, I feel a sense of closeness and sense of freedom. The best thing about collaboration is the fact that it requires one to let go of control, because one works together with their writing partner to create a piece that you can't predict. The final outcome of the piece is my favorite part, getting to see how two different voices come together in this surreal space.

A writer who might want to seek out this kind of connection should be open to any writing-related opportunities that come their way. Find out about any local workshops taking place, or readings at your local (indie) bookshops. Reach out to writers whose work resonates with you: you never know what can happen after just one small meaningful interaction. If you're lucky enough to join an MFA program, take advantage of all the resources offered to you; you'll likely befriend people in the program.

Another of our recent *Driftwood Press* authors, Winshen Liu, whose book *Paper Money* won our latest chapbook contest, uses Chinese characters in her work. She explained her choice to not translate these by saying that though she is writing in English, her goal was not to write for the "White Gaze." The Asian American writer Ananya Vahal urges writers not to "whitewash" their stories, and in an interview for PBS's *American Masters*, Toni Morrison said, "I have spent my entire writing life trying to make sure that the white gaze was not the dominant one in any of my books." Was this something you were also thinking about in your choice to move between languages as you do? How would you advise a non-Span-

ish-speaking reader to approach your book, especially the poem(s) where Spanish is central?

Yes, in line with Liu, Vahal, and Morrison, resisting the white gaze was definitely an approach I'd actively been considering while moving between languages. My goal wasn't to translate my text for the reader, as not only would it disrupt the text in a way that wouldn't aesthetically align with my work, but it wouldn't stay true to the words on the page, the way that some Spanish can't be translated completely. Additionally, it's extra emotional labor that I feel I don't need to be performing for my monolingual speakers. I would advise a non-Spanish-speaking reader to confront my book, especially the poems where Spanish is central, to listen to the rhythm, the sound, the way the letters look on the page. Of course, there is always taking the time to Google translate everything, but since even my Spanish is experimental, just experiencing the poem rather than trying to understand its meaning would be the most satisfying way to access these pieces.

Research is so important in this collection. The poet Helen Rickerby wrote that in poetry, "Facts are never just facts; they are always serving some kind of symbolic or subtextual purpose." What is your process like when you utilize factual material from other sources? Where do you think this impulse comes from for you? What do you think the function of historical or factual information/other voices is in a poem?

Incorporating research is a really important process throughout much of my work; to fuel an image or to even get to a starting point many times, I start by using the online etymology dictionary, to help me expand my understanding and find new ways of looking at a certain word or phrase, for example. My process for completing the research portion of this specific collection involved looking up factual links, like you would for a research paper, starting by exploring many different sources, eventually narrowing them down, and finding approaches to incorporating the language into poetic material, like a puzzle .

I took a Documentary Poetics course with an important mentor, Holly Iglesias, while in my master's program, and this is where the impetus for research came about. I think in general, my impulse for research comes from my natural exploratory character, as someone who loves to learn more and always wants to answer and solve those complicated, philosophical questions. I think the function of historical or factual information / other voices in a poem is to provide another perspective, to preserve history, to highlight voices that may have been left in the background in more common historical texts and narratives. I always go back to Natasha Trethewey's *Bellocq's Ophelia* as a pivotal text that delves into those voices, those that might have otherwise been silenced if it weren't for the writer bringing them forward and out onto the page.

I am also interested in the way you use italics. Sometimes you italicize Spanish words, sometimes English, sometimes neither. To me, this feels connected to the idea of interruption, in your poems, of multiple voices. Do you see italics as directly connected to those intersections in language?

You're right, I mainly use italics to emphasize voice(s). Much of the italics are used for either internal dialogue, or to highlight the dialogue of others. Sometimes I italicize Spanish words, to accent rhythm, for example, when I italicize the song lyrics in "Moon as Salted Lemon". This also creates interruption / has readers immersing themselves in two different worlds: one of the scene in which the speaker is by themselves, at a bar, as if the Julieta Venega's "Limón y Sal" were playing in the background, but the song also take readers into a different landscape, a sensation that reaches the emotions of moonlit dusk.

I do believe that italics serve a connection to these intersections in language—I think it's common for people to italicize a different language in their poetry to distinguish between English and Spanish, for example, but I find that to be distracting and not serving the poem in a way that can demonstrate its full potential if the other language were to stand on its own. Of course, everyone has their own style, but I think that finding the voices instead, and really digging deep into the interruptions, to italicize that which *really* deserves this type of stress, can make for a really interesting and layered piece.

Yet another pivotal and complex thing this book does is to educate readers about the diversity in the Jewish community. I was not completely familiar with Sephardic Jewish history and culture (likely for reasons you discuss in these poems!), and I found the cultural element so fascinating, especially considering cultural biases and antisemitism (and on the other hand, Zionism) that are constantly part of our American news and media cycles. I wonder if there is anything more you would like us to know about your family and/or your connection to Judaism now—how close are you to your speaker, in this regard? Also, are there resources you could recommend to our readers, if they'd like to learn more?

My connection to Judaism has always been complicated; I grew up going to Hebrew school, a place that was not a friendly environment for me for so many reasons. My dad (the Sephardic side of my family) is quite religious; when we were younger, he tried to get us to keep Shabbat (no using electronics, no going out on Friday nights), until he eventually gave up. I think writing documentary poetics gave me an outlet / the space to connect with my Jewish heritage in a way I wasn't able to before. In this way, I think I became closer to the speaker while writing these poems (during the time I was writing some of these poems, my ex-partner also helped me connect to the more spiritual side of Judaism: I started to focus less on how I needed to practice being a Jew and more engaging in activities that feel more meaningful to me, such as understanding the connection between tarot and Kabbalah, for example, or spending time celebrating Shabbat with my friends; most importantly, when I'm able to find the intersection that holds both my queerness and religion together, I'm in a liberating space whereby I can start believing a little bit more in a higher power again.

Some resources I've learned about that are related to Sephardic Judaism are thanks to my friend Emanuel Ovadia (@gdframbuaz): Diarna.org, which is a digitizing project of Jewish spaces in SWANA (Southwest Asia and North Africa).

RedJuderias.org offer descriptions and travel guides of former Jewish quarters in Spain. This page is really good for showing the Jewish history in Spain. Most of the content is in Spanish, but the travel guides themselves are usually bilingual.

The American Ladino League is a new org to promote Ladino in the US and preserve the history of the language here. They often have webinars with cool Sephardi and Ladino personalities, and they also have a weekly all-level Ladino Zoom room.

The University of Washington has a digital Sephardic studies collection, where folks can explore digitized letters, newspapers, amulets, photos, passports, and more by Sephardi folks.

I am so drawn to the ways your sparse lines and experimental language evoke a strong sense of place, from Madrid to Miami. Was it important to you that your readers felt physically transported in this book? To me, this feels so deeply connected to the concept of exile. No place feels safe.

I'm so glad that you picked up on the nuances of place! Sometimes, I feel like quite a bit of my poems seem to transcend place, but I really did want to evoke the physicality of each space, especially that of Madrid and Miami. It's also important that you bring the concept of exile to the forefront—Spain historically was not a safe place for Jews, though I still have family living there now, and to me, it's a second home. I think what this sentiment brings up is the idea of conflict in a place one lives in: As someone who has lived in Miami for most of my life, I have a strong long-enduring love-hate relationship to it: a humid, car-reliant, expensive-to-the-bones city, where everything is spread out. And yet, it's also a city where one can live in sunshine all the time, there is nature quite unlike anywhere else, and the beaches, of course…but we can also refer back to the segregation of Jews in these same locations, in Miami Beach specifically, for example.

What advice do you have for our readers about how to capture place in a poem? Is it important that a poet have deeply rooted connections to the place they are trying to capture?

Capturing a place in a poem can be tricky and very abstract sometimes, as depending on our relationship to place, the way in which we illustrate it will change with time. I think one way to begin writing about place, as cliché as this may sound, is to start off with a childhood memory and work your way from the more physical sensations of place to that of the more sensorial. What emotions come about when you think about the air outside the patio in your childhood home? What was it like to skate on the gravelly pavement of your neighborhood's cul-de-sac?

I don't think it's necessarily required that a poet have a deeply rooted connection to a place they are trying to capture, but perhaps the nuance might be lost if they haven't spent enough time in that one specific place they are writing about. One can write about feeling estranged from a place, for example, and that is an intimate form of connection, as that love-hate relationship I mentioned before most likely will arise when describing your sense of location and the heartbreak that can come with it.

In the long poem "Sephardic Shabbos Starved," you talk about, "Cuisine as control./ Diet as restraint," you call this, "Galactosemic." Your speaker seems to be chained to culture by food, whereas the brother "gets out." The speaker, then, does gain (false?) control at the end through disorder. There seems to be such a tug of war here, between wanting to claim an identity outside of the family (especially with the juxtaposition of your more personal/more historic sections) and wanting history and culture not to be erased. Food is such a beautiful and arresting symbol for this. How can we strike out to find our

individual identity while fighting bias and erasure of cultures, perhaps even cultures which would erase other parts of our identity? How did you approach writing about something so complex and difficult?

Wow, this is such a nuanced question, and you absolutely touched upon so many significant points, such as that of restriction, food, culture, and history. I wanted to honor Sephardic culture, and its rituals while also acknowledging the ways in which cultural norms, especially around gender and the body can be suffocating. There's a desire to preserve history and also a need to carve out an independent self. The speaker internalized control through an eating disorder. I think a lot of marginalized people, especially those who hold multiple, conflicting, identities, experience this kind of push-and-pull—between belonging and self-definition, between survival and erasure.

With regards to how we can find out individual identities while fighting bias and erasure of cultures, even cultures which would erase other parts of our identity: I think it's about reclaiming agency in ways that don't require self-destruction. This might mean finding ways to reinterpret or practice tradition / culture, find communities that intersect with other identities that are more inclusive, and engaging in conversation that uplifts culture rather than erasing it.

Your collection ends with the poem "Linguistic Rewilding," with a note directly crediting Gloria Anzaldua and "salvaje." Could you explain, if you wish to, the concept of salvaje to readers who may not be familiar? How is this central to the collection? What made you want to make this the last poem in the collection? And, to take it broader, what do you think the function of the "final poem" is in a poetry collection?

In Gloria Anzaldúa's "How to Tame a Wild Tongue", the first scene she writes about is the speaker at the dentist's; the dentist is performing a procedure on her. He tells her, "We're going to have to control your tongue". The concept of "controlling one's tongue" usually refers to controlling the way in which one speaks. In this way, the tongue is seen as "salvaje", or "wild". I actually learned about the concept of rewilding while I was observing a class in my master's program (rewilding is a conservation strategy that restores natural processes and ecosystems to allow nature to thrive).

I find the concept of "salvaje" central to my collection because much of it deals with the "wild" in many different ways and in many various iterations of what that word might mean: "wild" as in "wild" in the sense of animalistic, "wild" in the more contemporary ways in which we use the word, wordplay a "wild" maze, through which readers are taken on a wild ride, and "wild" as in speaking out, without restraint.

I wanted this to be the last poem in the collection because it feels like a powerful piece that requires a lot of space and breathing room, one last punch for readers to get hit by. I wished to end on a note that touched on the concept of poignancy and language and how those two work together, because so much of my collection is about that idea but is not stated as explicitly as it is in this final piece. I think the function of the "final poem" in a poetry collection is to leave readers either satisfied, in awe, or wanting more.

I am confident readers will be both satisfied by this collection, and they will want to see more from you! As a final question, then, what's next for you?

I've been tinkering with a chapbook that highlights pop cultural references and emo / punk culture a little bit more, changing the tone from that of more serious to maybe what I would consider a breathing space after this collection (though the chap still includes themes of mental illness, but more subtly so). My next full-length collection is tentatively titled "Boundary Work", an extension of my piece "Why Are There Boundaries"; working on boundaries has basically been a life-long journey for me, and something I'd like to process within and onto the page. I also hope that within the next year or so, I'll be invited to do a lot more readings and workshops.

NOTES

"Lemon as Etrog / The Growth and Swallow of a Jewish Mom's Phenomenological Body" (pg. 6):
Etrog is the yellow citron used during Jewish Sukkot holiday. The act of shaking the lulav (palm branch) and etrog are together is a mitzvah which helps to bring the person offering the blessing closer to God. These items also kabastically represent a person's body parts (the lulav symbolizes the spin and the Etrog embodies the heart).

Martha Rosler's "Semiotics of the Kitchen" is a feminist parody and performance piece that was released in 1975 and which critiques commodified versions of traditional women's roles in society, such as that of replacing the sound and usage of domesticated kitchen tools with the language of rage.

"Hungering over / Solidifying into Succade" (pg. 24):
Succade is the candied peel of any of the citrus species, especially the citron. In order to understand the multiple meanings as well as phenomenological implication / importance behind the title, it may be important to note the fact that "succade" may have originated from the Hebrew word sukkah, which is a temporary hut, or shelter, that Jews usually eat in during the Sukkot holiday.

"Why Are There Boundaries" (pg. 52):
This poem is inspired by / borrows its title from FKJ's song with the same name.

"Ex Nihilo (Exilio)" (pg. 55):
This section break references two poems by Shmuel HaNagid (Samuel ibn Naghrillah), a medieval Spanish Talmudic scholar, grammarian, politician, and influential poet who was born in Córdoba, Spain. He was known as a great writer who not only knew Hebrew and Latin, but also mastered the Arabic language. The excerpts / epigraphs included in this section are translated (from the medieval Hebrew) by Peter Cole.

"Stateless" (pgs. 56-57):
The first stanza / lines, "Of course, Spain / was not a country / for immigrants", the sixth stanza / lines "[…] To admit / Jews was to attack the very essence of Span / ish / ness", and the twelfth through thirteen stanzas, "*In the late nineteenth century / [….] knowledge of Jews / among the*

majority / of Spaniards was non- / existent" are all taken from Michael Alpert's article (from Jewish Historical Studies) titled "Dr. Angel Pulido and Philo-Sephardism in Spain".

In the sixteenth stanza, the line *"is it time for the Jews / to leave / Europe?"* is taken from the title of Jeffrey Goldberg's *The Atlantic* article, published in 2015.

"Kabbalistic Hauntings" (pgs. 60-61):
The italicized phrase, "There is, in fact, a widespread / hesitation, to describe Jews / as Jews" is taken from Mark Oppenheimer's *[The] New York Times* opinion article titled "Reclaiming Jew".

The information / lines in the twelve and thirteenth stanzas ("In 1950, there were more than / A quarter of a million Jews / In Morocco, but today / there are maybe 2,000, / in the big urban areas / of Casablanca and Marrakech"), as well as the (modified) line, "the old country / remembers us", are taken from Sarah Mamlet Rabat's *IES Abroad* blog article titled "What Remains: Discovering the Traces of Jewish Life in Morocco".

"Blood Libel" (pgs. 62-64):
The italicized words and phrases are taken from *The Atlantic*'s article title "Spain's Attempt to Atone for a 500-Year-Old Sin".

Salvador Espriu was one of the great Catalonian poets and novelists of the 20th century, who came of age during the Spanish Civil War and Franco dictatorship.

"Matar judíos" is the name of a Spanish tradition/lemonade drink that is consumed in in the village of León during Easter. "The name is believed to come from medieval time when converted Jewish people were sometimes publicly executed at show trials around Easter in Spain" (*The Independent*, "Spanish village called 'kill Jews' considers name change").

"Dream Phaneron" (pg. 64):
This section break includes another poem by Shmuel HaNagid ("He'll Bring You Trouble"), which I've chosen to speak in conversation with a more contemporary poet, Muriel Rukeyser, an American poet and political activist, most known for her poems about feminism, social justice, and Judaism. The theme of dream is one I wanted to focus on towards this last portion, to provide a bit of "breathing space" between the heavier poems and those more focused on a more personal liberation, in a sense.

Rukeyser's poem is titled "Phaneron", which is a philosophical theory of phenomenology, introduced by Charles Sanders Pierce, an idea of "being", or presence, or as defined as "phenomenon" in the way it meant "whatever is present at any time to the mind in any way". This idea seems to complement the fields of psychoanalysis, metaphysics, and dream theory quite well.

This section break title, or concept, is also a nod / coincidentally relates to the anthology titled "Dream of the Poem: Hebrew Poetry from Muslim and Christian Spain, 950-1492" (Lockert Library of Poetry in Translation), (or even more contemporarily, so does Adrienne Rich's "Dream of a Common Language").

"Linguistic Rewilding" (pgs. 75-78):
The concept of "salvaje" is taken from Gloria Anzaldúa's essay "How to Tame a Wild Tongue".

ACKNOWLEDGEMENTS

Grateful acknowledgement is made to the editors of the following publications, in which some of these poems / pieces, or versions of them, originally appeared:

"Balanceando", "No Me Importa un Pimiento", "The Fucked up Part about Fucking You" *Limp Wrist*, 2022

"Bioluminescent Insomnia", "Surreal Architectures" *The Hooghly Review*, 2023

"Category Theory" *Kissing Dynamite Press*, 2020

"Hornbone Season," "Nasophilia," "When a Dream Speaks to Me," "Thrum" *Pussy Magic*, 2020

"La Fábul(os)a" *Reflex Press*, 2020

"Lemon: A Prelude", "7 Ingredient (Way to Wish for Someone's Just Dessert) Lemon Bar Recipe" *Olney Magazine*, 2022

"Linguistic Rewilding/ Rebobinas Linguísticos" Academy of American Poets (Alfred Boas Poetry Prize), 2019

"Moon as Salted Lemon" *SWWIM Every Day*, 2020

"Nimble / Thimble Touch" *SWWIM Every Day*, 2021

"Qué Guay" *Third Coast Magazine*, 2025

"Sleight of Hand", "Panic Attack", "Orange Somatics" *Crêpe & Penn*, 2020

"Ser la Leche" *Grist Journal*, 2021

"When the Root of Apple (תפוח) Sweetly Exhales", "Ars Poetica #___" *ANMLY*, 2021

Photography: Vanessa Diaz

Clayre Benzadón (she / they) is a queer (bi /pan) Sephardic-Ashkenazi poet, educator, and activist. Her chapbook, *Liminal Zenith*, was published by *SurVision Books* in 2019. Her manuscript *Moon as Salted Lemon* was recently named an honorable mention for Miami Book Fair's 2025 Emerging Writer's Fellowship. She has been published in places including *Jet Fuel Review, Libre,* and *SWWIM*. Find more about her here: https://www.clayrebenzadon.com.

OTHER DRIFTWOOD PRESS TITLES

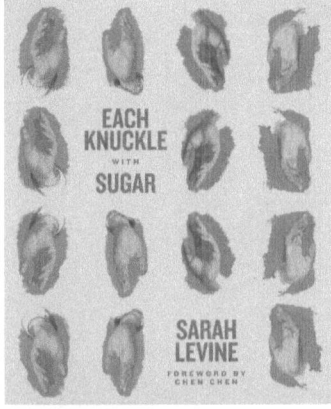

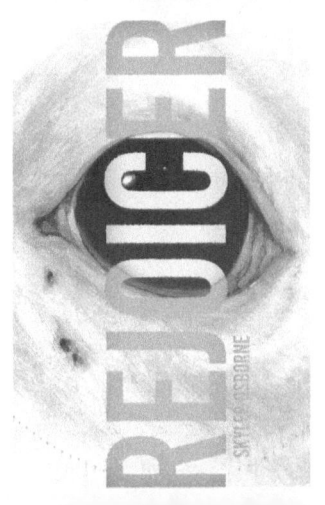

www.ingramcontent.com/pod-product-compliance
Lightning Source LLC
Chambersburg PA
CBHW060531080526
44586CB00012B/703